Compiled by
Dan Zadra with Susan Scott

Designed by
Kobi Yamada and Steve Potter

brilliance

Uncommon voices from uncommon Women.

COMPENDIUM
INCORPORATED

live inspired.

ACKNOWLEDGEMENTS
The author of the Brilliance™ collection wishes to express his sincere appreciation to Seattle writer, lecturer and business consultant Susan Scott whose seminars and workshops are widely acclaimed. Susan's seminar brochure describes her simply as "a pebble kicker for women." Her remarkable track record as a consultant for some of America's most dynamic young companies proves she also moves mountains.

WITH SPECIAL THANKS TO
Jason Aldrich, Gloria Austin, Gerry Baird, Jay Baird, Neil Beaton, Josie Bissett, Laura Boro, Chris Dalke, Jim and Alyssa Darragh & Family, Jennifer and Matt Ellison & Family, Rob Estes, Michael and Leianne Flynn & Family, Sarah Forster, Jennifer Hurwitz, Heidi Jones, Carol Anne Kennedy, June Martin, Jessica Phoenix and Tom DesLongchamp, Janet Potter & Family, Diane Roger, Kirsten and Garrett Sessions, Kristel Wills, Clarie Yam and Erik Lee, Heidi Yamada & Family, Justi and Tote Yamada & Family, Bob and Val Yamada, Kaz and Kristin Yamada & Family, Tai and Joy Yamada, Anne Zadra, August and Arline Zadra, and Gus and Rosie Zadra.

CREDITS
Compiled by Dan Zadra with Susan Scott
Designed by Kobi Yamada and Steve Potter

ISBN: 978-1-932319-20-0

3rd Printing. 5K 02 08   Printed in China

Thoughts To Inspire & Celebrate
Your Achievements™

Here's to you and to "Brilliance"

Brilliance may be difficult to describe, but we all know
it when we see it. It's a bright idea, a daring decision,
an ingenious insight, a soaring aspiration, or a wise
and compassionate action.

"Brilliance is one part talent, two parts wisdom and
three parts passion," wrote Pulitzer Prize winning novelist
Margaret Mitchell. "Whenever you encounter it in your
midst, celebrate it, encourage it, be happy for it."

This little book is one way of doing just that. It's a treasury
of wise and wonderful quotations–a celebration of life,
love and work–from some of the most creative and
accomplished women of our times.

brilliance

"Brilliance" is not so much a book about women as it is a
book about life through a woman's eyes. It celebrates and
encourages some of the best parts of the human spirit–our
everyday cares, concerns and commitments, our dreams,
hopes and plans, our mistakes, setbacks and triumphs.

We hope we have created a book that both men and women
will savor, treasure and keep. We think you'll soon discover,
however, that the real joy and satisfaction comes from giving
it away. Look around. Someone in your midst is brilliant.
Celebrate them. Encourage them. Be happy for them.

THE FUTURE BELONGS
TO THOSE WHO BELIEVE
IN THE BEAUTY OF
THEIR DREAMS.

–Eleanor Roosevelt

Reality is something you rise above.

–LIZA MINNELLI

I might have been born
in a hovel, but I was determined
to travel with the wind and the stars.

–JACQUELINE COCHRAN

Longing performs all things.

–MARY RENAULT

brilliance

Uncommon voices from uncommon Women.

We know not where our dreams
will take us, but we can probably see quite
clearly where we'll go without them.

–MARILYN GREY

When nothing is sure, everything is possible.

–MARGARET DRABBLE

Dreams come a size
too big so that we can grow into them.

–JOSIE BISSETT

If one is lucky,
a solitary fantasy can totally transform
one million realities.

–MAYA ANGELOU

We couldn't conceive
of a miracle if none had ever happened.

–LIBBIE FUDIM

Reach high, for stars
lie hidden in your soul. Dream deep,
for every dream precedes the goal.

–PAMELA STARR

brilliance

Uncommon voices from uncommon women.

If I had influence with the
good fairy, I would ask that her gift
to each child be a sense of wonder
so indestructible that it would
last throughout life.

–RACHEL CARSON

Hope is the thing with feathers
that perches in the soul, and sings
the tune without the words,
and never stops at all.

–EMILY DICKINSON

Begin doing what you
want to do now. We are not living in
eternity. We have only this moment,
sparkling like a star in our hand–
and melting like a snowflake.

–MARIE BEYNON RAY

If it's a good idea, go ahead and do it.
It is much easier to apologize than
it is to get permission.

–ADMIRAL GRACE MURRAY HOPPER

brilliance

Uncommon voices from uncommon Women.

It takes as much
energy to wish as it does to plan.

–ELEANOR ROOSEVELT

When people keep telling you
that you can't do a thing,
you kind of like to try it.

–MARGARET CHASE SMITH

Action is the antidote to despair.

–JOAN BAEZ

You can't wring
your hands and roll up your sleeves
at the same time.

–MICHELE BROWN

What the hell–you might
be right, you might be wrong…
but don't just avoid.

–KATHARINE HEPBURN

You may be disappointed
if you fail, but you are doomed
if you don't try.

–BEVERLY SILLS

brilliance

Uncommon voices from uncommon women.

To believe in something
not yet proved and to underwrite it
with our lives; it is the only way
we can leave the future open.

–LILLIAN SMITH

Get off the sidewalk.
Walk the street with us into history.

–DOLORES HUERTA

brilliance

Uncommon voices from uncommon Women.

Be courageous.
It's one of the only places
left uncrowded.

—Anita Roddick

And the trouble is,
if you don't risk anything, you risk even more.

–ERICA JONG

You gain strength, courage
and confidence by every experience in which
you really stop to look fear in the face. You
must do the thing you think you cannot do.

–ELEANOR ROOSEVELT

I was always looking outside myself
for strength and confidence, but it comes
from within. It is there all the time.

–ANNA FREUD

Security is mostly a superstition.
It does not exist in nature. Life is either
a daring adventure or nothing.

–HELEN KELLER

My favorite thing is to go
where I've never been.

–DIANE ARBUS

You cannot advance
when you concentrate on retreat.

–SUE SIKKING

brilliance

Uncommon voices from uncommon Women.

It is not easy to be a pioneer–
but oh, it is fascinating! I would not trade
one moment, even the worst moment,
for all the riches in the world.

–ELIZABETH BLACKWELL

Courage is the price
that life exacts for granting peace.

–AMELIA EARHART

brilliance

Uncommon voices from uncommon Women.

The essential
conditions of everything
you do must be choice,
love, passion.

–Nadia Boulanger

Find the passion.
It takes great passion and great energy
to do anything creative. I would go so far as
to say you can't do it without that passion.

–AGNES DEMILLE

Passion is not
necessarily something we have,
it's something we choose.

–SUSAN SCOTT

Life loves
to be taken by the lapel and told,
"I'm with you kid. Let's go."

–MAYA ANGELOU

One can never
consent to creep when one feels an
impulse to soar.

–HELEN KELLER

Talent is a flame. Genius is a fire.

–B. WILLIAMS

brilliance

Uncommon voices from uncommon women.

When in doubt, make a fool of yourself.
There is a microscopically thin line between
being brilliantly creative and acting like
the most gigantic idiot on earth.
So what the hell, leap!

–CYNTHIA HEIMEL

Choose life!
Only that and always! At whatever risk.
To let life leak out, to let it wear away by the
mere passage of time, to withold giving and
spending it…is to choose nothing.

–SISTER HELEN KELLY

When the world laughs at you, laugh back.
It's just as funny as you are.
–THOMASINA HORTON

I'm the foe of moderation,
the champion of excess. I'd rather be
strongly wrong than weakly right.
–TALLULAH BANKHEAD

It's better to be a lion
for a day than a sheep all your life.
–SISTER ELIZABETH KENNY

brilliance

Uncommon voices from uncommon women.

For the sake
of making a living we forget to live.

–MARGARET FULLER

Life is too short to short yourself on life.

–TERRI ZADRA

That's our function in life–
to make a declarative statement.

–CORINNE JACKER

If you are not
afraid to die, why be afraid to live?

–JOANNA SPARKS

Life is in the here and now,
not in the there and afterwards.
This day, with all the travail and joy that
it brings to our doorstep, is the expression
of eternal life. Eithcr we meet it,
we live it–or we miss it.

–VIMALA THAKAR

brilliance

Uncommon voices from uncommon women.

Earth is crammed with heaven.

–ELIZABETH BARRETT BROWNING

I don't want to get
to the end of my life and find that I just lived
the length of it. I want to have lived
the width of it as well.

–DIANE ACKERMAN

Adventure is worthwhile in itself.

–AMELIA EARHART

brilliance

Uncommon voices from uncommon women.

Cherish forever
what makes you unique,
'cuz you're really a
yawn if it goes!

–Bette Midler

Why compare
yourself with others?
No one in the entire world can
do a better job of being
you than you.

–SUSAN SCOTT

Never compromise yourself.
You are all you've got.

–BETTY FORD

He who walks
in another's tracks leaves no footprints.

–HELEN OTTWAY

You are unique, and if
that is not fulfilled, then something
has been lost.

–MARTHA GRAHAM

We relish news of our heroes,
forgetting that we are extraordinary
to somebody too.

–HELEN HAYES

brilliance

Uncommon voices from uncommon Women.

Self-respect has nothing to do
with reputation or the approval of others.

–JOAN DIDION

It's nice to be included
in people's fantasies, but you also like
to be accepted for your own sake.

–MARILYN MONROE

Some of the most important things
in life aren't things.

–LINDA ELLERBEE

It's easy to be independent
when you've got money. But to be
independent when you haven't got
a thing–that's the Lord's test.

–MAHALIA JACKSON

I'll keep my personal dignity and
pride to the very end. It's a possession
that only I myself can part with.

–DAISY BATES

brilliance

Uncommon voices from uncommon Women.

The best and most
beautiful things in the world
cannot be seen or even touched.
They must be felt with the heart.

–HELEN KELLER

I would rather
have roses on my table than
diamonds on my neck.

–EMMA GOLDMAN

The more you get,
the more you got to take care of.

–ALICE DORMANN

It's amazing how many cares
one loses when one decides not to be
something, but to be someone.

–COCO CHANEL

Until you've lost your reputation,
you never realize what a burden it was
or what freedom really is.

–MARGARET MITCHELL

brilliance

Uncommon voices from uncommon Women.

Don't confuse fame with success.
Madonna is one; Helen Keller is the other.

–ERMA BOMBECK

I've begun to think of myself
as "independently wealthy" because
I realize that I carry within myself most
of what I need to make me happy.

–CATHLEEN ROUNDTREE

How we spend our days is,
of course, how we spend our lives.

–ANNIE DILLARD

brilliance
Uncommon voices from uncommon Women.

When you get
into a tight place and it
seems that you can't go on,
hold on—for that's just the
place and the time that
the tide will turn.

–Harriet Beecher Stowe

Life is not easy
for any of us. Early on in life
I decided that I would not be
vanquished and that I would remain
cheerful in the face of circumstances.

–ROSE KENNEDY

You can't be brave
if you've only had wonderful
things happen to you.

–MARY TYLER MOORE

You have to have faith
that there is a reason you go through
certain things. I can't say I am glad to go
through pain, but in a way one must,
in order to gain courage and really feel joy.

–CAROL BURNETT

One thing I learned the hard way
was that it doesn't pay to get discouraged.
Keeping busy and making optimism a way
of life can restore your faith in yourself.

–LUCILLE BALL

brilliance

Uncommon voices from uncommon women.

There are two ways of
meeting difficulties. You can alter
the difficulties, or you can alter
yourself meeting them.

–PHYLLIS BOTTOME

No life is so hard that you can't make
it easier by the way you take it.

–ELLEN GLASGOW

The way I see it, if you want
the rainbow, you gotta
put up with the rain.

–DOLLY PARTON

Laughter in the face of reality
is probably the finest sound there is. In fact,
a good time to laugh is any time you can.

–LINDA ELLERBEE

Experience is pure gold.
Experience is what you get when
you don't get what you want.

–ANN LANDERS

I thank God for my handicaps,
for through them I have found myself,
my work and my God.

–HELEN KELLER

brilliance

Uncommon voices from uncommon women.

Having it all doesn't
necessarily mean having it all at once.

–STEPHANIE LUETKEHAUS

The force of the waves is
in their perseverance.

–GILA GURI

You may have to fight a battle
more than once to win it.

–MARGARET THATCHER

Be patient.
Our prayers are always answered,
but not always on the exact day
we'd like them to be.

–MARJORIE TURNER

Comedy is tragedy plus time.

–CAROL BURNETT

Just pray for a tough hide
and a tender heart.

–RUTH GRAHAM

brilliance

Uncommon voices from uncommon women.

God doesn't give breaks.
He gives breakthroughs.

–JUNE MARTIN

I know God will not give me
anything I can't handle. I just wish
that He didn't trust me so much.

–MOTHER TERESA

I make the most of all
that comes and the least
of all that goes.

–SARA TEASDALE

I don't look at what I've lost.
I look instead at what I have left.

–BETTY FORD

So much has been give to me;
I have no time to ponder over that
which has been denied.

–HELEN KELLER

Just don't give up trying to do
what you really want to do. Where there
is love and inspiration, I don't think
you can go wrong.

–ELLA FITZGERALD

brilliance

Uncommon voices from uncommon Women.

Success doesn't come to you. You go to it.

–Marva Collins

Anyone who says the days
of opportunity are over is copping out.

–ANN LANDERS

Winners have the ability to adapt
to the terrain. They take responsibility
for their own career path.

–MARY CUNNINGHAM

It is more important
to know where you are going than
to get there quickly. Never mistake
activity for achievement.

–MABEL NEWCOMBER

brilliance

Uncommon voices from uncommon women.

The first duty of a human being
is to find your real job and do it.

–CHARLOTTE PERKINS GILMAN

No one can arrive from being
talented alone. God gives talent;
work transforms talent into genius.

–ANNA PAVLOVA

I don't wait for moods. You accomplish
nothing if you do that. Your mind must
know it has got to get down to earth.

–PEARL S. BUCK

Some people regard discipline
as a chore. For me, it's a kind of
order that sets me free to fly.

–JULIE ANDREWS

My success was not based so much
on any great intelligence but on
great common sense.

–HELEN GURLEY BROWN

Champions take responsibility.
When the ball comes over the net,
you can be sure I want the ball.

–BILLIE JEAN KING

brilliance

Uncommon voices from uncommon women.

The person who knows
"how" will always have a job. The person
who knows "why" will always be his boss.

–DIANE RAVITCH

Be prepared.
It's better to have it and not need it,
than to need it and not have it.

–ELIZABETH ANN NOLAN

The formula for success is simple:
Do your best and someone might like it.

–MARVA COLLINS

Doing your best
at this moment puts you in the
best place for the next moment.

–OPRAH WINFREY

When we do the best we can,
we never know what miracle is wrought
in our life, or in the life of another.

–HELEN KELLER

brilliance

Uncommon voices · from uncommon Women.

It's amazing how lucky
I become whenever I consistently put out
my best effort.

–CYBIL FRANKLIN

Luck means the hardships you have
not hesitated to endure; the long nights
you have devoted to your work.
Luck means the appointments you have
never failed to keep, the airplanes
you never failed to catch.

–MARGARET CLEMENT

I was born to shiver
in the draft from an open mind.
–PHYLLIS MCGINLEY

Innovators are inevitably controversial.
–EVA LE GALLIENNE

Creative minds
have always been known to survive
any kind of bad training.
–ANNA FREUD

brilliance

Uncommon voices from uncommon women.

It's a mistake to surround
yourself only with people just like you.
Throw off that worn comforter—
and replace it with a crazy quilt
of different and imaginative people.
Then watch the ideas erupt!

–BETTY BENDER

Imagination is the
highest kite you can fly.

–LAUREN BACALL

Excellence makes people nervous.

–SHANA ALEXANDER

No man or woman who tries
to pursue an ideal in his or her own way
is without enemies.

–DAISY BATES

If I'm too strong for some people,
that's their problem.

–GLENDA JACKSON

brilliance

Uncommon voices from uncommon women.

Being powerful is like being a lady.
If you have to tell people you are, you aren't.

–MARGARET THATCHER

The key to whatever success I enjoy
today is: Don't ask. Do.

–VIKKI CARR

Self-reliance is the answer
to the question, "Who can I turn to?"

–PATRICIA SAMPSON

It's amazing how
fast doors open to us when we dare
to take control of a situation.
–CATHERINE PONDER

Doubt who you will, but never yourself.
–CHRISTINE BOVEE

Instead of this absurd division
into sexes they ought to class people
as static and dynamic.
–EVELYN WAUGH

brilliance

Uncommon voices from uncommon women.

If at first you don't succeed,
you're probably lucky.
–MARGARET L. CLEMENT

The fame you earn
has a different taste from the fame
that is forced upon you.
–GLORIA VANDERBILT

I climbed the ladder
of success wrong by wrong.
–MAE WEST

Mistakes are a part
of the dues one pays for a full life.

–SOPHIA LOREN

Show me a person who has never
made a mistake and I'll show you somebody
who has never achieved much.

–JOAN COLLINS

We ought to be able to learn some
things second-hand. There is not enough
time for us to make all the mistakes ourselves.

–HARRIET HALL

brilliance

Uncommon voices from uncommon women.

A mistake is simply
another way of doing things.

I'll match my flops with anybody's
but I wouldn't have missed them. Flops are a
part of life's menu and I've never been one
to miss out on any of the courses.

brilliance
Uncommon voices from uncommon women.

There are people
who take the heart
out of you, and
there are people
who put it back.

–Elizabeth David

Those who are lifting
the world upward and onward are
those who encourage more than criticize.

–ELIZABETH HARRISON

The best index to a person's character
is how he treats people who can't do him
any good–and how he treats people
who can't fight back.

–ABIGAIL VAN BUREN

Appreciation in any form
at any time brightens anyone's existence.

–RUTH STAFFORD PEALE

Sandwich every bit of criticism
between two layers of praise.

–MARY KAY ASH

Listening, not imitation,
is the sincerest form of flattery.

–JOYCE BROTHERS

brilliance

Uncommon voices from uncommon women.

As novices, we think we're
entirely responsible for the way
people treat us. I have long since
learned that we are responsible only
for the way we treat people.

–ROSE LANE

Expect people to be better
than they are; it helps them
to become better. But don't be
disappointed when they are not;
it helps them to keep trying.

–MERRY BROWNE

Ideas are a dime a dozen,
but the men and women who
implement them are priceless.

–MARY KAY ASH

If you have a company,
hire children to sit on your board.
Then listen and learn. Their instincts
are excellent. They cherish lived-up-to
promises and real guarantees.

–FAITH POPCORN

brilliance

Uncommon voices from uncommon Women.

You cannot manage men
into battle. You manage things;
you lead people.

–ADMIRAL GRACE MURRAY HOPPER

Never doubt that
a small group of thoughtful,
committed people can change
the world. Indeed, it is the
only thing that ever has.

–MARGARET MEAD

I don't think you should
ever manage something that
you don't care passionately about.

–DEBORAH COLEMAN

I keep an eye on the bottom line,
but it's not an overriding obsession. To me,
P and L doesn't just mean "profit and loss"–
it also means "people and love."

–MARY KAY ASH

brilliance

Uncommon voices from uncommon Women.

What matters today is
not the difference between those
who believe and those who do not believe,
but the difference between those
who care and those who don't.

–ABBE PIRE

If the future is to remain
open and free, we need people who
can tolerate the unknown, who will not
need the support of completely worked-
out systems or traditional blueprints
from the past.

–MARGARET MEAD

Everybody wants
to do something to help, but
nobody wants to be first.

–PEARL BAILEY

Concern should drive us
into action and not into a depression.

–KAREN HORNEY

Those who think
they have no responsibilities are those
who have not sought them out.

–MARY LYON

brilliance

Uncommon voices from uncommon women.

You have not lived
a perfect day, even though you
have earned your money, unless you
have done something for someone
who will never be able to repay you.

–RUTH SMELTZER

The only thing that makes
one place more attractive to me
than another is the quantity
of heart I find in it.

–JANE WELSH CARLYLE

The history of every country
begins in the heart of a man or a woman.

–WILLA CATHER

This I know. This I believe with
all my heart. If we want a free and
peaceful world, if we want to make deserts
bloom and man to grow to greater dignity
as a human being–we can do it!

–ELEANOR ROOSEVELT

These are the hard times in which
a genius would wish to live. Great necessities
call forth great leaders.

–ABIGAIL ADAMS

brilliance

Uncommon voices from uncommon women.

After the verb
"To Love"…"To Help"
is the most beautiful
verb in the world.

–Bertha von Suttner

What the world
really needs is more love
and less paperwork.
–PEARL BAILEY

The human heart,
at whatever age, opens to the
heart that opens in return.
–MARIE EDGEWORTH

If you have knowledge,
let others light their candles at it.
–MARGARET FULLER

brilliance

Uncommon voices from uncommon Women.

The fragrance always
stays in the hand that gives the rose.

–HADA BEJAR

Blessed are those
who can give without remembering
and take without forgetting.

–ELIZABETH BIBESCO

The heart that gives–gathers.
–HANNAH MOORE

To give without any reward,
or any notice, has a special
quality of its own.
–ANNE MORROW LINDBERGH

'Twas her thinking of others
made you think of her.
–ELIZABETH BARRETT BROWNING

brilliance

Uncommon voices from uncommon women.

Empathy is
your pain I feel in my heart.

–HOSPICE VOLUNTEER

Since when do you have
to agree with people to defend
them from injustice?

–LILLIAN HELLMAN

The greatest achievements are those
that benefit others.

–LILLIAN GILCREST

We must have places
where children can have a whole group
of adults they can trust.

–MARGARET MEAD

I think leaders should
encourage the next generation not just
to follow, but to overtake.

–ANITA RODDICK

Light tomorrow with today.

–ELIZABETH BARRETT BROWNING

brilliance

Uncommon voices from uncommon women.

Never mistake
knowledge for wisdom.
One helps you make a living;
the other helps you
make a life.

–Sandra Carey

I have learned a philosophy
in the great University of Hard Knocks.
I have learned to live each day as it comes,
and not to borrow trouble
by dreading tomorrow.

–DOROTHY DIX

If only we'd stop trying to be happy,
we could have a pretty good time.

–EDITH WHARTON

Worry is a misuse of the imagination.

–AUDREY WOODHALL

brilliance

Uncommon voices from uncommon women.

If something is wrong, fix it
if you can. But train yourself not to worry.
Worry never fixes anything.

–MARY HEMINGWAY

Advice is what we
ask for when we already know the answer
but wish we didn't.

–ERICA JONG

The best advice
yet given is that you don't have to take it.

–LIBBIE FUDIM

Think wrongly, if you please,
but in all cases think for yourself.

–DORIS LESSING

You can never get yourself
or anybody else into trouble by being honest.

–ROSE LANE

My dog and cat
have taught me a great lesson
in life…shed a lot.

–SUSAN SCOTT

brilliance

Uncommon voices from uncommon women.

One loses so many
laughs by not laughing at oneself.

–SARA JEANNETTE DUNCAN

There is always something
left to love. And if you ain't learned that,
you ain't learned nothing.

–LORRAINE HANSBERRY

You grow up the day
you have your first real laugh–at yourself.

–ETHEL BARRYMORE

God always has
another custard pie up his sleeve.

–LYNN REDGRAVE

Believe there is a great power
silently working all things for good, behave
yourself and never mind the rest.

–BEATRIX POTTER

Never let the urgent
crowd out the important.

–KELLY CATLIN WALKER

brilliance

Uncommon voices from uncommon women.

The main thing
is to keep the main thing
the main thing.

–KELLY ANN ROTHAUS

Time is a very precious gift
from God; so precious that it is only
given to us moment by moment.

–AMELIA BARR

For fast-acting relief try slowing down.

–LILY TOMLIN

I believe there are more urgent
and honorable occupations than
the incomparable waste of time
we call suffering.

–COLETTE

Never face facts; if you do
you'll never get up in the morning.

–MARLO THOMAS

brilliance

Uncommon voices from uncommon women.

When you make a mountain
out of a molehill, you have to climb it.

–SUE SIKKING

The perception of a problem
is always relative. Your headache
feels terrific to the druggist.

–RAMONA E. F. ARNETT

As important as "hanging on"
is knowing when to "let go."

–SHERRI DEWITT

brilliance

Uncommon voices from uncommon women.

If you obey
all the rules you miss
all the fun.

–Katharine Hepburn

A little of what
you fancy does you good.

–MARIE LLOYD

Here's a rule I recommend.
Never practice two vices at once.

–TALLULAH BANKHEAD

Between two evils, I always pick
the one I never tried before.

–MAE WEST

Lead me not into temptation;
I can find the way myself.

–RITA MAE BROWN

Let's face it. Some mistakes
are too much fun to only make once.

–GLORIA PORTMAN

My life is full of mistakes.
They're like pebbles that make a good road.

–BEATRICE WOOD

brilliance

Uncommon voices from uncommon women.

If you always do
what interests you, then at least
one person is pleased.

–KATHARINE HEPBURN

Happiness is something that comes
into our lives through doors we
don't even remember leaving open.

–ROSE LANE

Joy seems to me a step
beyond happiness. Happiness is a sort of
atmosphere you can live in sometimes when
you're lucky. Joy is a light that fills you with
hope and faith and love.

–ADELA ROGERS ST. JOHNS

You will do foolish things,
but do them with enthusiasm.

–COLETTE

brilliance

Uncommon voices from uncommon women.

Love doesn't make
the world go 'round.
Love is what makes
the ride worthwhile.

–Carol Burnett

I thing we're here for each other.

–CAROL BURNETT

You can't be human alone.

–MARGARET KUHN

I want to love first,
and live incidentally.

–ZELDA FITZGERALD

brilliance

Uncommon voices from uncommon women.

There is time for work.
And time for love. That leaves no other time.

–COCO CHANEL

When you love someone,
all your saved-up wishes start coming out.

–ELIZABETH BOWEN

Love is a game that two can play
and both can win.

–EVA GABOR

Love is like fresh bread.
It has to be re-made all the time,
made new.

–URSULA K. LEGUIN

Familiarity,
truly cultivated, can breed love.

–DR. JOYCE BROTHERS

If you love someone,
then hurry up and show it.

–ROSE ZADRA, AGE 6

brilliance

Uncommon voices from uncommon women.

Expressed affection is
the best of all methods to use when
you want to light a glow in someone's
heart and to feel it in your own.

–RUTH STAFFORD PEALE

One of the oldest human needs
is having someone wonder where you are
when you don't come home at night.

–MARGARET MEAD

The motto should not be,
"Forgive one another."
Rather, "Understand one another."

–EMMA GOLDMAN

Never go to bed mad. Stay up and fight.

–PHYLLIS DILLER

Trouble is a part of life, and
if you don't share it, you don't give
the person who loves you a chance
to love you enough.

–DINAH SHORE

brilliance

Uncommon voices from uncommon women.

Go ahead and cry. I'll catch your tears.

–JILEEN RUSSELL

People change
and forget to tell each other.

–LILLIAN HELLMAN

If you haven't forgiven yourself
something, how can you forgive others?

–DOLORES HUERTA

We lose a lot of time hating people.

You cannot
shake hands with a clenched fist.

Love your enemies–it will
drive them nuts.

brilliance

Uncommon voices–from uncommon Women.

Love people.
Use things. Not vice-versa.
–KELLY ANN ROTHAUS

My friends are my estate.
–EMILY DICKINSON

It's the friends you can
call up at 4 A.M. that matter.
–MARLENE DIETRICH

You never know
when you're making a memory.

–RICKIE LEE JONES

Lots of people want
to ride with you in the limo,
but what you want is someone
who will take the bus with you
when the limo breaks down.

–OPRAH WINFREY

You are loved.
If so, what else matters?

–EDNA ST. VINCENT MILLAY

brilliance

Uncommon voices from uncommon women.

Turn around and
you're two, turn around and
you're four, turn around and
you're a young girl going
out of my door.

—Malvina Reynolds, "Turn Around," 1958

We mothered this nation. And we have
no intention of abandoning our roles as
nurturer or wife, mother, loving daughter,
tax-paying citizen, homemaker, breadwinner.

–LIZ CARPENTER

Motherhood is still the biggest gamble
in the world. It is the glorious life force.
It's huge and scary–it's an act of
infinite optimism.

–GILDA RADNER

brilliance

Uncommon voices from uncommon women.

Making the decision to have a child–
it's momentous. It is to decide forever to have
your heart go walking around outside your body.

–ELIZABETH STONE

I saw pure love when my son looked
at me, and I knew that I had to make
a good life for the two of us.

–SUZANNE SOMERS

At work you think of the children at home.
At home you think of the work you've
left undone. The struggle within
yourself tears at the heart.

–GOLDA MEIR

A mother is a person who,
seeing there are only four pieces of pie
for five people, promptly announces
she never did care for pie.

–TENNEVA JORDAN

We didn't have much but we sure had plenty.

–SHERRY THOMAS

The walks and talks we have with our two-
year-olds in red boots have a great deal to do
with the values they will cherish as adults.

–EDITH F. HUNTER

brilliance

Uncommon voices from uncommon women.

The real menace in dealing with
a five-year-old is that in no time at all
you begin to sound like a five-year-old.

–JEAN KERR

To grown people a girl of fifteen
is a child still; to herself she is very old
and very real; more real, perhaps,
than ever before or after.

–MARGARET WIDDEMER

You have to love your children unselfishly.
That's hard, but it's the only way.

–BARBARA BUSH

Parents learn a lot from their
children about coping with life.

–MURIEL SPARK

There's a lot more to being a woman
than being a mother, but there's
one hell of a lot more to being a mother
than most people suspect.

–ROSEANNE BARR

I learned so much more about
men by having a son.

–BARBRA STREISAND

brilliance

Uncommon voices from uncommon Women.

We want our children to fit in and
to stand out. We rarely address the
conflict between these goals.

–ELLEN GOODMAN

The elders still say: "You know
I have been young, but you can never have
been old." But today's kids can reply:
"You've never been young in the world
I am young in, and you never can be."

–MARGARET MEAD

We had a disappointing experience with
our children–they all grew up.

–LESLIE BONAVENTURE

No matter how old a mother is
she watches her middle-aged children
for signs of improvement.

–FLORIDA SCOTT-MAXWELL

Your children are always your babies,
even if they have gray hair.

–JANET LEIGH

Choose to have a career early
and a family late. Or choose to have a family
early and a career late–but plan a long life.

–DR. JANET ROWLEY

brilliance

Uncommon voices from uncommon women.

It is never too late
to be what you
might have been.

–George Eliot

Life is a process of becoming,
a combination of states we have to
go through. Where people fail is
that they wish to elect a state
and remain in it.

–ANAIS NIN

You may have a fresh start
any moment you choose, for
this thing that we call "failure"
is not the falling down, but
the staying down.

–MARY PICKFORD

brilliance

Uncommon voices from uncommon women.

You should always know
when you're shifting gears in life.
You should leave your era;
it should never leave you.

–LEONTYNE PRICE

The final forming
of a person's character
lies in their own hands.

–ANNE FRANK

When I was growing up I always
wanted to be someone. Now I realize
I should have been more specific.

–LILY TOMLIN

The trouble with life is, you're
halfway through it before you realize
it's a "do it yourself" thing.

–ANNIE ZADRA

brilliance

Uncommon voices from uncommon women.

Every human being
on this earth is born with the tragedy
that he has to grow up. A lot of people
don't have the courage to do it.

–HELEN HAYES

I think somehow we learn
who we really are and then live
with that decision.

–ELEANOR ROOSEVELT

Do you know why grown-ups
are always asking little kids what they want
to be when they grow up? It's because
they're looking for ideas.

–PAULA POUNDSTONE

Life is what happens to you
when you are making other plans.

–BETTY TALMADGE

brilliance

Uncommon voices from uncommon women.

In the long run, we shape our lives
and we shape ourselves. The process never
ends until we die. And the choices we make
are ultimately our responsibility.

–ELEANOR ROOSEVELT

You can have the results you say
you want, or you can have all the reasons
why you can't have them. But you can't
have both. Reasons or results.
You get to choose.

–SUSAN SCOTT

Adventure is something you seek for pleasure, or even profit, like a gold rush; but experience is what really happens to you in the long run–the truth that finally overtakes you.

–KATHERINE ANNE PORTER

If the future road looks ominous or unpromising, and the roads back uninviting, then we need to gather our resolve and, carrying only the necessary baggage, step off that road into another direction.

–MAYA ANGELOU

brilliance

Uncommon voices from uncommon women.

Age is
not important
unless you're
a cheese.

–Helen Hayes

I am not a has-been. I'm a will be.

–LAUREN BACALL

Sooner or later I'm going to die,
but I'm not going to retire.

–MARGARET MEAD

We turn not older with years,
but newer every day.

–EMILY DICKINSON

brilliance

Uncommon voices from uncommon women.

I believe in hard work.
It keeps the wrinkles out of the mind
and the spirit. It helps to keep a
woman going.

–HELENA RUBENSTEIN

In a word, I am always busy,
which is perhaps the chief reason
why I am always well.

–ELIZABETH CADY STANTON

You never grow old
until you've lost all your marvels.

–MERRY BROWNE

The older I grow, the more I listen
to people who don't say much.

–GERMAIN GLIDDEN

I shall not grow conservative with age.

–ELIZABETH CADY STANTON

brilliance

Uncommon voices from uncommon women.

Life is the first gift;
love is the second;
and understanding
is the third.

–MARGE PIERCY

I look forward
to growing old and wise
and audacious.

–GLENDA JACKSON

If you rest, you rust.

–HELEN HAYES

Regret is an appalling
waste of energy. You can't build on it;
it's only good for wallowing in.

–KATHERINE MANSFIELD

One's prime is elusive.

–MURIEL SPARK

brilliance

Uncommon voices from uncommon Women.

I have no regrets.
I wouldn't have lived my life the way
I did if I was going to worry about
what people were going to say.

–INGRID BERGMAN

What a lovely surprise
to discover how unlonely
being alone can be.

–ELLEN BURSTYN

You can take no credit
for beauty at sixteen. But if you
are beautiful at sixty, it will be
your soul's own doing.

–MARIE STOPES

You know, of course,
that it is never too late to begin.
Why, Grandma Moses didn't start
her painting career until she
was seventy-six!

–CARRIE BETHARD

brilliance

Uncommon voices from uncommon women.

Beauty is not caused. It is.

–EMILY DICKINSON

I love my past.
I love my present. I'm not ashamed
of what I've had, and I'm not sad
because I have it no longer.

–COLETTE

We are always the same age inside.

–GERTRUDE STEIN

If I had my life to live over,
I'd like to make more mistakes next time.
I would climb more mountains and swim
more rivers. I would eat more ice cream
and less beans. I would perhaps have more
actual troubles, but fewer imaginary ones.

–NADINE STAIR, AGE 81

brilliance

Uncommon voices from uncommon women.

It seems to me
we can never give up longing
and wishing while we are alive. There are
certain things we feel to be beautiful and
good, and we must hunger for them.

–GEORGE ELIOT

What a wonderful life I've had.
I only wish I'd realized it sooner.

–COLETTE

brilliance

Uncommon voices from uncommon women.